For Rosiân, Ennis,
and Tristan with love.

*From Snowflakes to Sandcastles* © Frances Lincoln Limited 1996
Text and illustrations copyright © Annie Owen 1996

Published in the United States in 1996 by
The Millbrook Press, Inc., 2 Old New Milford Road
Brookfield, Connecticut 06804

First published in Great Britain by
Frances Lincoln Limited, 4 Torriano Mews
Torriano Avenue, London NW5 2RZ

Printed and bound in Hong Kong

1 3 5 7 9 8 6 4 2

**Library of Congress Cataloging-in-Publication Data**
Owen, Annie.
From Snowflakes to Sandcastles : a child's year in words and pictures / by Annie Owen.
p.   cm.
Summary : Pictures illustrate thirteen words
for each month of the year. Includes questions
prompting the reader to search for and find various objects.
ISBN 1-56294-086-4 (lib. bdg.)   ISBN 1-56294-269-7 (trade)
1. Vocabulary--Juvenile literature.  [1. Vocabulary.  2. Months.
3. Picture puzzles.]  I. Title.
PE1449.085  1995    95-10535
428. 1--dc20    CIP
AC

# From Snowflakes to Sandcastles

## A Child's Year in Words and Pictures

# Annie Owen

The Millbrook Press
Brookfield, Connecticut

# January

snowballs ★ gloves flashlights

snowflakes ★ mittens ★ boots slippers

scarves wool hats ★ snowmen

hot-water bottles snowdrops ★ moon

Can you find two spotted mittens?

Which glove is the odd one out?

Where are the blue slippers?

How many snowmen can you see?

Is there a wool hat that looks like yours?

**What else can you see in January?**

# February

hearts ♥ crocuses ★ pancakes

teddy bears ★ coats ★ earmuffs

pajamas ★ ice skates muffins

toboggans icicles ★ jam ★ toast

How many pairs of ice skates can you find?

What is your favorite teddy wearing?

Which coat do you like best?

Can you find two pancakes that are filled with jam?

How many valentine hearts are there?

**What else can you see in February?**

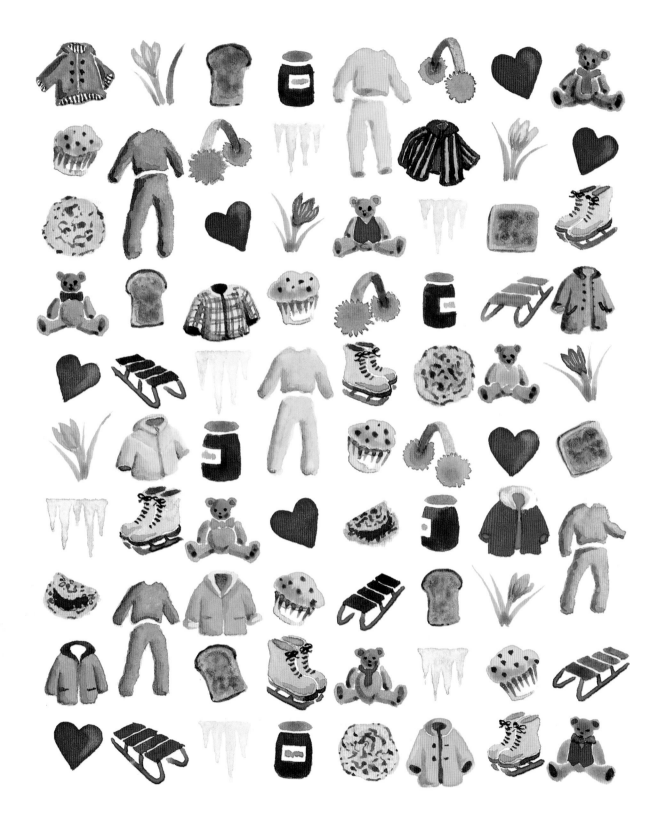

# March

tadpoles ★ windmills ★ puppies

daffodils

toy cars ★ overalls

jackets ★ sneakers

pencils

dolls ★ birds' nests

frogs ★ sweaters

Is there a jacket just like yours?

How many different crayons are there?

Can you find a doll with red shoes?

Where are the yellow overalls?

Can you spot the tadpole that has grown legs?

**What else can you see in March?**

# April

raindrops * umbrellas * strollers

lambs * primroses * rainbows * grass

Easter eggs * clouds * ducklings

rubber boots * rain hats * bunnies

How many ducklings can you find?

Which Easter egg do you wish you could eat?

Are all the lambs the same color?

Can you find five strollers?

One of the rubber boots has fallen over. Where is it?

**What else can you see in April?**

# May

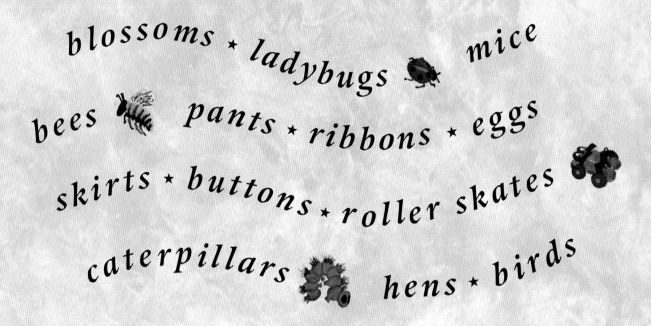

blossoms ★ ladybugs mice

bees pants ★ ribbons ★ eggs

skirts ★ buttons ★ roller skates

caterpillars hens ★ birds

How many pink buttons can you count?

Can you spot the hen with her chicks?

What color is the longest ribbon?

Is the green caterpillar hairy?

Which ladybug has the most spots?

**What else can you see in May?**

# June

kites *buttercups* ★ *daisies*

*lollipops* ★ *frisbees* ★ *shorts* bats

*T-shirts* ★ *butterflies* sandals

*strawberries* *baseball caps* ★ *balls*

Can you find two kites with faces?

Which butterfly do you think is the prettiest?

How many T-shirts can you count?

Where is the strawberry with a bite out of it?

What color is your favorite lollipop?

**What else can you see in June?**

# July

streamers · masks ★ potato chips

pom-poms ★ party hats ♕ popsicles

hot dogs ★ balloons fireworks ★ flags

drums ★ trumpets hamburgers

Where is the strawberry-flavored popsicle?

Are all the trumpets exactly the same?

Can you see the balloon that has burst?

How many hot dogs have mustard on them?

Which party hat would you like to wear?

**What else can you see in July?**

# August

sunshine ★ buckets 🪣 starfish

beach balls ★ spades ★ ice cream cones

deck chairs 🏖 sandcastles ★ seaweed

crabs 🦀 sunhats ★ swimsuits ★ shells

Which sunhat is your favorite?

How many starfish can you count?

What color is the seaweed?

Can you find the striped shorts?

Which sandcastle has a purple flag?

**What else can you see in August?**

# September

pears ★ school bags 🎒 bananas

apples 🍎 thunderclouds ★ honey

lightning ★ sunflowers ★ books ★ corn

tractors ★ socks 🧦 new shoes

Which shoes have yellow laces?

How many books are there? Are you sure?

Can you find two peeled bananas?

Which socks have red and yellow patterns?

Where is the forked lightning?

**What else can you see in September?**

# October

broomsticks ⋆ trees ⋆ nuts bats

candy ⋆ squirrels ghosts

witches candy apples ⋆ leaves

lanterns ⋆ pumpkins chestnuts

How many leaves can you count?

Which ghost is the scariest?

Can you spot the pumpkin with a face?

Can you find the candy apple with a bite missing?

Where is the witch's cat?

**What else can you see in October?**

# November

footballs * owls cranberries
puddles * turkeys * spiders stars
planets Pilgrim hats * geese
apple pies * bonfires cobwebs

Can you count the Pilgrim hats?

Which apple pie has ice cream on top?

Are all the owls awake?

Can you find two purple planets?

How many cobwebs have spiders on them?

**What else can you see in November?**

# December

Christmas trees ★ holly ★ presents

Santa Kwanzaa cup ★ ornaments

menorahs ★ angels Kwanzaa candles

tinsel ★ cards ★ dreidels ★ stockings

Can you find the angel in the golden dress?

Which present looks most exciting?

Where is Santa?

How many dreidels can you count?

Can you find a Kwanzaa cup?

**What else can you see in December?**